Contents

Shadow Creatures 1

Spot-Bellied Eagle-Owl 6

Indian Giant Flying Squirrel 10

Hump-Nosed Pit Viper 14

Indian Hedgehog 18

Short-Nosed Fruit Bat 22

Malabar Spiny Dormouse 26

Common Palm Civet 30

Himalayan Newt 34

Ghost Crabs 38

Red Sand Boa 42

Spot Them Here! 46

Fact Finder and Credits 47

Shadow Creatures

Have you ever wondered what the animals around you are up to while you're fast asleep? As the sun starts setting and you eat dinner, the owls emerge, hooting and hunting. While you stay cosy under the covers, snakes slither out of their burrows, starting the search for food. Your dreams might echo the screeches of bats, flapping furiously through the night skies. There's a whole world shrouded in shadows, so read along to find out what might go bump in the night.

Why Do Some Animals Avoid the Sun?

It's pretty easy for us human beings to beat the heat. Sunscreen, a cool soda, a fan or an air conditioner are ways we modify our environments to keep our bodies at a normal temperature. Animals, especially cold-blooded ones, don't have this luxury. Many tropical animals rest during the day and come out at night to avoid the sun and prevent overheating. Dehydration and sunstroke are no joke.

The Indian giant flying squirrel, found in the Western Ghats

Is it Easier to Find Dinner in the Dark?

A moonlit dinner means something different for the hunter and the hunted. Animals like lions sometimes hunt during the night because their prey, like zebras and antelopes, have poor night vision. This makes them easier to catch. Other animals like field mice are active during the night because their predators roam the skies during the day. Who knew when you go to bed could be the difference between staying safe or becoming someone's dinner?

The hump-nosed pit viper, found in India and Sri Lanka

How Do Animals See in the Dark Without a Flashlight?

Nocturnal animals have a whole host of senses to help them survive in the dark. Their eyes are entirely different from ours. While colour is vital to help us navigate the world, it matters less to nocturnal animals. Their priority is trying to absorb as much light as possible. Nocturnal animals usually have very large, wide eyes that don't see too much colour. Many animals also rely on their nose. A sharp sense of smell can be much more reliable in the dark.

Are Nocturnal Animals in Trouble?

Unfortunately, a lot of nocturnal animals are threatened by human activities. The biggest problem is light pollution. When there's bright light all day and night, animals get confused about when to wake up, go to sleep or start looking for food. Lots of night creatures use the moon and stars to find their way, but city lights can block the night sky, making it hard for them to navigate. It's important for humans to adopt practices that protect night-time animals.

The spiny dormouse is found only in the southern Western Ghats

Spot-Bellied Eagle-Owl

Find Me Here!

The Western and Eastern Ghats, and occasionally as far north as Uttarakhand and even Northeast India.

CRITTER STATS

Scientific name: *Ketupa nipalensis*
Size: 50–65 cm tall – the size of a backpack. Their wingspans can reach up to 1.7 m.
Weight: 1.5–2.5 kg
Lifespan: unknown
Habitat: dense deciduous forests
Conservation status: least concern

The aptly named spot-bellied eagle-owl is a fierce predator, coming alive at night. Adult eagle-owls are majestic creatures, with menacing, eyebrow-like "tufts" jutting out from the side of their heads. Deep black eyes help them see as they quietly fly through the forest.

During the day, you'd be hard-pressed to find an eagle-owl hidden in the leaves of the dense forests that they live in. As the sun sets, the magnificent bird comes alive.

They perch upon tall branches, and their multicoloured feathers help them camouflage into the dark browns and blacks of a night-time forest.

The eagle-owl waits patiently, scanning the forest floor. Its eyes have evolved to gather even the faintest light, allowing them to see with clarity in almost complete darkness.

Its feathers are layered, ensuring that they fly silently. In one quiet swoop, they extend talons and catch their prey.

The eagle-owl punches way above its weight. It's been documented to take down peafowl, pheasants and even mouse deer! Mouse deer weigh almost twice as much as the eagle-owl.

DID YOU KNOW?

Sri Lankan legends tell stories of a "devil bird", with a human-like screech. Some researchers think that the owl's unique call has earned it this nickname.

The spot-bellied eagle-owl is the only eagle-owl which lays a single egg every breeding season. This single egg is also unusually large, matching those of the world's biggest eagle-owl species!

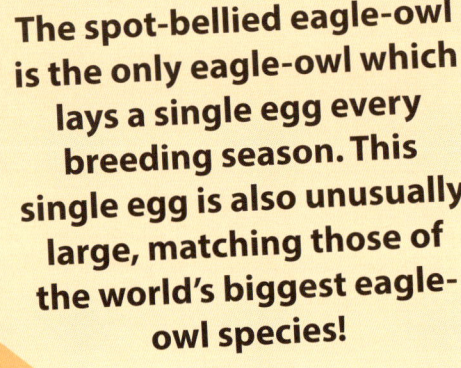

Some researchers believe that the owl's tufts help it communicate with other birds, much like how our eyebrows convey facial expressions! They are usually upright when hunting.

Indian Giant Flying Squirrels

Find Me Here!

Found in the Western Ghats and in scattered pockets across central India.

CRITTER STATS

Scientific name: *Petaurista philippensis*

Size: the body is around 43 cm – the size of a loaf of bread. The tail can be 0.5 m.

Weight: up to 1.65 kg

Lifespan: unknown

Habitat: forest edges and plantations

Conservation status: least concern

If you walk through a dark forest, you'll undoubtedly hear a symphony of sounds. You may also hear an odd series of rustles. Could it be the Indian giant flying squirrel, journeying from tree to tree?

The fluffy, reddish-brown body of the Indian giant flying squirrel is tricky to catch a glimpse of in the night-time. Instead, you might spot its large, glistening eyes or its long, dark tail dangling from the treetops.

Between its front and back legs, this squirrel has a built-in parachute. This thin, furry membrane is known as the patagium. It helps catch air, carrying it from treetop to treetop.

Gliding allows them to travel quickly and look for food efficiently. It could also help them make a quick escape from predators.

Like other nocturnal animals, this squirrel has big eyes. Sharp eyesight helps the flying squirrel find its favourite fruits, like ficus, figs and jackfruit.

This fruit-lover plays an important role in spreading seeds all over the forest.

DID YOU KNOW?

The Indian giant flying squirrel prefers short glides, but its speed is unmatched. They have been documented to reach speeds of 43 km/h!

They often fight over holes and hollows in the trunks of old trees, choosing only the best ones to nest in.

While adults rely on their eyesight to navigate the inky skies, baby squirrels are born blind. They open their eyes only after a few weeks.

Hump-Nosed Pit Viper

Find Me Here!

The hump-nosed pit viper is found only in the Western Ghats of India and across Sri Lanka!

CRITTER STATS
Scientific name: *Hypnale hypnale*
Size: 30–45 cm long – like a steering wheel
Weight: around 150 g
Lifespan: unknown
Habitat: dense jungles and coffee plantations
Conservation status: not evaluated

The hump-nosed pit viper's exceptional camouflage conceals its striking beauty from all but the most observant eyes. True to its name, this secretive reptile sports a distinctive upturned snout.

This snake hides in leaf litter, creeping onto sun-warmed rocks to snooze.

Between its eyes and nostrils lie heat-sensing organs known as "pits". These pits function like built-in thermal cameras, detecting nearby animals.

Small creatures are detected by their heat signatures alone, even in complete darkness.

The snake's body is a mottled dark brown. It blends in perfectly with dry, decaying leaves. During the daytime, it hides in plain sight.

The hump-nosed pit viper is more a sprinter than a marathon runner. It's generally considered a slow mover, lying in wait for prey. When it pounces, it can be lightning quick.

DID YOU KNOW?

The rattlesnake might be famous for shaking its tail, but it's not the only snake to do so. When irritated, the hump-nosed pit viper shows annoyance by shaking its tail and flattening its body.

For a long time, scientists thought this venomous snake was relatively harmless. Now, they know it's responsible for the highest number of recorded snakebites in Sri Lanka!

Pit vipers often flick their tongues in the air. This is because they smell through their tongues!

Indian Hedgehog

Find Me Here!
Found primarily along the western edges of India, in the drier regions of Gujarat and Rajasthan.

CRITTER STATS

Family: *Paraechinus micropus*
Size: about 17 cm – the size of a TV remote
Weight: 300–400 g
Lifespan: unknown
Habitat: sandy deserts, dry and rocky areas
Conservation status: least concern

Try waking up an Indian hedgehog during the day, and you'll quickly meet its prickly personality – and spines! By day, the Indian hedgehog snoozes in a cosy burrow, hidden from the heat. Come nightfall, it waddles out on tiny feet, ready to explore.

Indian hedgehogs look like tiny, spiky footballs. Their back spines typically lie flat. When hedgehogs get scared, they stand on end, giving the animal its iconic prickly appearance.

These resourceful creatures live in some of India's hottest regions, using their nocturnal habits to avoid scorching temperatures.

Mother hedgehogs also give birth to pups inside these underground dens, where they remain safe from predators and don't overheat.

As darkness falls, hedgehogs emerge as opportunistic foragers, consuming an amazing variety of prey – insects, beetles, worms, slugs, eggs and even venomous scorpions!

When threatened, they curl up into a ball, with spines on the outside. This formidable armour keeps them safe from predators.

DID YOU KNOW?

Indian hedgehogs are super into skincare. When they taste or smell something unfamiliar, they spread saliva onto their spines and fur. Scientists aren't quite sure why they display this quirk, though it could be for scent marking.

Any open burrow is fair game for the Indian hedgehog! They often steal burrows that other animals have dug.

It takes baby hedgehogs three weeks to learn how to open their eyes, but they can roll into a ball to protect themselves as young as one week old!

Short-Nosed Fruit Bat

Find Me Here!

The short-nosed fruit bat is found all across the Indian subcontinent.

CRITTER STATS

Scientific name: *Cynopterus sphinx*
Wingspan: 48 cm – like a computer keyboard
Weight: 60 g
Lifespan: unknown, likely around 10 years
Habitat: tropical forests and orchards
Conservation status: least concern

As dusk falls, short-nosed fruit bats awaken and fly out in search of ripe treats. Big eyes, a stubby nose and fluffy fur makes them look like puppies with wings. Their love for fruit ensures they play a vital role in nature by spreading seeds and helping forests grow.

At the end of this bat's short snout is its most important organ: the nose! Short-nosed fruit bats have an extremely powerful sense of smell.

They can distinguish between ripe and unripe fruits, different types of fruits, and even identify friends and foes with their scent. The nose knows!

The short-nosed fruit bat also prefers to hang out with company. During the day, eight or nine bats all roost together.

As night falls, you might see groups of bats waking up and heading out from their roosts together. They stay in touch with loud, screechy calls.

DID YOU KNOW?

Short-nosed fruit bats have an incredible appetite. They can eat more than their body weight in fruit in a single night! No wonder they hang upside down – it's probably the only way to digest an all-you-can-eat fruit buffet every night!

They trim leaves and stems of palms to size, and tie them together to make tents. They then nest in these tents.

"Eat dirt" isn't an insult for the short-nosed fruit bat. They regularly munch on soil and mud to get much needed minerals and salts.

Malabar Spiny Dormouse

Find Me Here!

Found only in the forests of the southern Western Ghats. It is found nowhere else in the world.

CRITTER STATS

Scientific name: *Platacanthomys lasiurus*
Size: 10–13 cm – as tall as a mug of coffee
Weight: 30–80 g
Lifespan: likely 2–4 years
Habitat: tropical evergreen forests
Conservation status: vulnerable

High in the rainy, misty Western Ghats is a region of mossy branches, dense forests and mists. Here lives the teeny-tiny spiny dormouse. This rodent is a master of the night-time forests, scurrying up and down trees with a grippy tail and strong feet.

With lush brown fur, tiny hand-like paws and big dark eyes, looking at one can make your heart melt.

But every adorable feature has a job. Those big eyes? They soak up as much light as possible, helping the dormouse sneak safely through the dark, tricky forest at night.

Its fur isn't just soft and cuddly. It's called "spiny" for a reason! Sharp, furry spines line its back like armour, protecting it from hungry predators.

Its hairy, long tail is as long (or longer) than its body! It ends in a tuft, like a lion's. Scientists think this helps them balance as they run up and down tree trunks.

The dormouse is also a voracious feeder. It holds fruits, nuts and seeds in its paws and makes quick work of them all.

DID YOU KNOW?

Plantation workers and owners aren't very fond of these creatures! They call them pepper rats for their ability to destroy large crops of pepper plants.

Farmers often collect toddy sap and leave pots of it to ferment. The spiny dormouse is famous for raiding these pots of toddy.

Not a lot is known about the mating behaviour of the spiny dormouse, but the females get very large during the wet season! Scientists think this is when they lay pups.

Common Palm Civet

Find Me Here!

The common palm civet is found all across India's forests.

CRITTER STATS

Family: *Paradoxurus hermaphroditus*
Size: 45–70 cm – a rolled up yoga mat
Weight: 2–5 kg
Lifespan: up to 25 years
Habitat: usually undisturbed forests
Conservation status: least concern

By day, the common palm civet is a rare sight. It vanishes into tree hollows or dense foliage. By night, this "civet cat" comes alive. Sleek and dark, it creeps through backyards, plantations and forests on silent feet. This creature is curious, clever and more than a little mysterious.

Common palm civets have dozens of names across Malaysia, India, Thailand and the other countries where they're found. Sometimes, it's called the "toddy cat" or "civet cat".

They are often found perched on palm trees, whose sap is used to make toddy, an alcoholic drink. Hence, the animal's name as well as its nickname!

*Image not from India

The palm civet relies on the white-fringed nose at the end of its snout. Its sense of smell helps it navigate the dark. It will eat almost anything, from bugs and beetles to fruits and seeds!

They are covered in different glands which release very, very strong scents. One of the most used glands is at the base of its tail. They mark trees, rocks and shrubs.

DID YOU KNOW?

Palm civets make the most expensive coffee in the world. Kopi luwak is a special coffee bean made from the poop of a palm civet that's eaten the coffee fruit!

Mother civets give birth to a litter of 2 to 5 babies. She makes sure to hide them in nests in tree hollows.

This animal has a sweet tooth and loves to eat fruit of the palm tree as well as honey.

Himalayan Newt

Find Me Here!

The Himalayan newt lives in West Bengal, Sikkim, Arunachal Pradesh and Manipur.

CRITTER STATS

Family: *Tylototriton verrucosus*
Size: 15–17 cm – the length of a notebook
Weight: 5–20 g
Lifespan: unknown
Habitat: ponds, swamps and streams
Conservation status: near threatened

With dark orange, knobbly skin, a flat head and a long tail, the Himalayan newt looks like a dinosaur in miniature. Part salamander, part mountain mystery, it thrives where few others dare to roam.

The Himalayan newt is a truly distinctive creature. As the only amphibian with a tail in the whole country, it represents a unique story in the book of evolution.

Mostly awake at night, it sneaks out under the cover of darkness to stay cool and hide from danger. It moves slowly through leaf piles and shallow ponds, gobbling up spiders, worms and even scorpions!

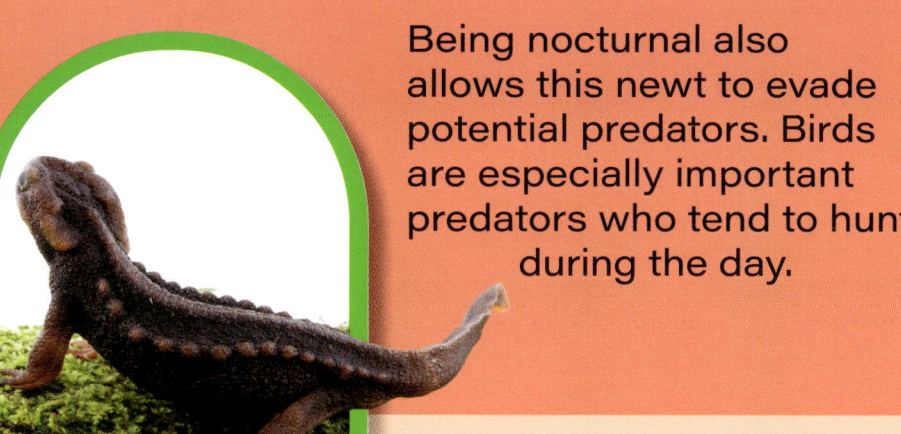

Being nocturnal also allows this newt to evade potential predators. Birds are especially important predators who tend to hunt during the day.

Male newts forgo dating apps and matrimonial websites for a much more elaborate courtship ritual. When a female approaches, the male rolls over, showing his bright orange belly. He also calls like a frog, luring the female to come closer.

Scientists know what it eats and where it lives, but there's still so much more to discover about this scientific mystery!

DID YOU KNOW?

The Nepalese word for the Himalayan newt is "paani kukur", which means "water dog". It makes a bark-like noise when it snaps its jaws.

Newts are unique because they lay eggs that hatch into tadpoles, similar to frogs and toads.

Some people call this newt the "crocodile newt", because of its unique, bumpy skin.

Ghost Crabs

Find Me Here!

Different types of ghost crabs are found all over India's coasts and beaches.

CRITTER STATS
Family: *Ocypodinae*
Length: 3.75–5 cm – like your index finger
Weight: 20–60 g
Lifespan: unknown
Habitat: sandy beaches
Conservation Status: not available

Walking on a beach at night feels like stepping into a dizzying optical illusion. The sand seems to come alive and scatter in a thousand different directions. These are ghost crabs, scurrying away from the pitter patter of noisy feet like tiny phantoms.

Ghost crabs get their spooky name because they sneak around the beach at night. Their see-through, whitish-yellow bodies help them vanish right into the sand!

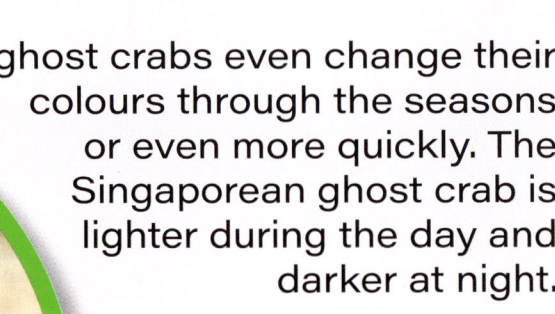

Some ghost crabs even change their colours through the seasons or even more quickly. The Singaporean ghost crab is lighter during the day and darker at night.

If ghost crabs went to college, they'd graduate as civil engineers. These ingenious creatures build their underground burrows at a 45-degree angle, facing the waves.

This design lets ocean breezes flow inside, keeping their homes cool. They can even cover their burrow entrances during the day with sand doors!

Ghost crabs aren't picky – they eat everything from eggs to human waste and to other smaller crabs. They also eat molluscs and worms.

 DID YOU KNOW?

Ghost crabs have eyes mounted on eye stalks. These eyes can swivel around, giving the crabs a 360-degree view of their surroundings.

The scientific name "*Ocypode*" means "fast feet". Ghost crabs can dart from side to side at 16 km/h on their tiny legs!

Ghost crabs make a wide variety of sounds to communicate with each other. They strike the sand with their claws, rub their legs together to make buzzes and even make bubbling noises with their gills.

Red Sand Boa

Find Me Here!

The red sand boa is found in western, north-western and southern India.

CRITTER STATS

Family: *Eryx johnii*
Length: 75–100 cm – the height of a toddler
Weight: 500–600 g, can grow to 3.5 kg
Lifespan: 14–20 years
Habitat: dry places and sandy soil
Conservation Status: near threatened

The red sand boa is a mysterious and rarely seen snake. It lives its life out of sight, emerging only in the night-time and living the days burrowed into the sand. Don't worry, it's not scary at all – just a gentle digger with a big secret: it's totally harmless!

With its smooth, reddish body sliding like water over the sand, it might just be the most beautiful member of the boa family!

If you catch a glimpse of its body, you might not be able to make head or tail of it! That's because the snake's tail is flattened at the tip to resemble a head.

This might be a clever adaptation to protect it from predators. They go for the tail instead of its head, leaving the most important bits alone.

The snake also prefers some of India's hottest desert habitats. It beats the heat by emerging only in the dark, when it prowls for prey like mice and lizards.

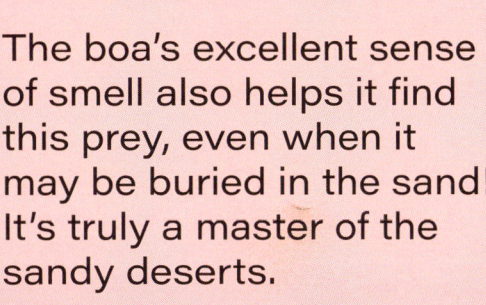

The boa's excellent sense of smell also helps it find this prey, even when it may be buried in the sand! It's truly a master of the sandy deserts.

 DID YOU KNOW?

The red sand boa is ovoviviparous. This means the eggs grow and hatch inside the mother's body! She then gives birth to live baby snakes.

The red sand boa is the largest sand boa in the world.

Its "two-headed" appearance has led to many superstitions. Some believe it will lead you to hidden treasure! Unfortunately, these superstitions have also caused illegal wildlife trade.

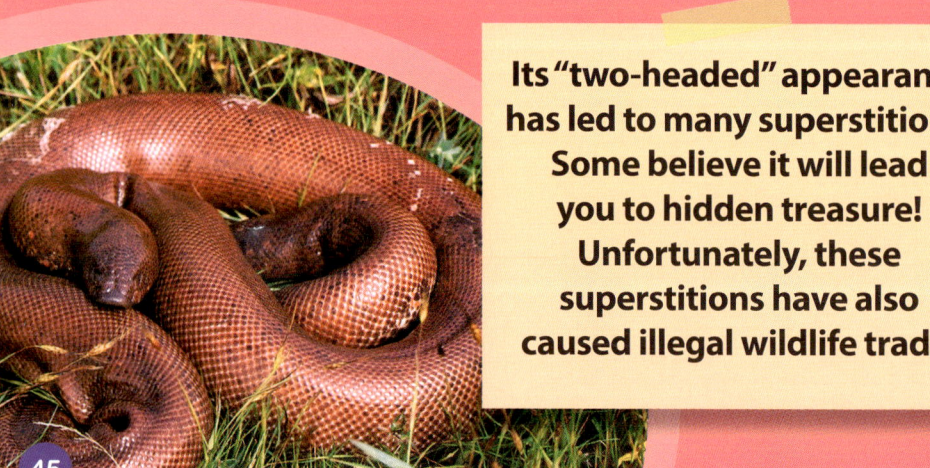

Spot Them Here!

Follow the pug marks to find some of the best places to spot India's amazing nocturnal wildlife!

Fact Finder

"Common Giant Flying Squirrel (Petaurista Philippensis)". *iNaturalist*, https://www.inaturalist.org/taxa/45984-Petaurista-philippensis.

"Common Palm Civet". *Nainital Zoo*, https://nainitalzoo.org.in/animal_details.php?cid=14.

"Ghost Crab: Facts, Diet, Habitat". *Roundglass Sustain*, https://roundglasssustain.com/infographics/ghost-crab-facts.

"Himalayan Newt". *Padmaja Naidu Himalayan Zoological Park*, https://darjeelingzoo.in/?tab=phnewt.

Holt, Denver W., et al. "Spot-Bellied Eagle-Owl (Ketupa Nipalensis), Version 1.1". *Birds of the World, 2022*. birdsoftheworld.org, https://doi.org/10.2173/bow.sbeowl1.01.1.

"Indian Hedgehog (Paraechinus Micropus)". *iNaturalist*, https://www.inaturalist.org/taxa/43065-Paraechinus-micropus.

Nandini, R. "Predation by Forest Eagle-Owl Bubo Nipalensis on Mouse Deer Moschiola Meminna". *Indian Birds, vol. 1, no. 5*, 2005.

Nirmal Kulkarni. "Hump-Nosed Pit Viper: Gem on the Forest Floor". *Roundglass Sustain*, https://roundglasssustain.com/species/hump-nosed-pit-viper.

"Paradoxurus Hermaphroditus (Asian Palm Civet)". *Animal Diversity Web*, https://animaldiversity.org/accounts/Paradoxurus_hermaphroditus/.

"Paraechinus Micropus (Indian Hedgehog)". *Animal Diversity Web*, https://animaldiversity.org/accounts/Paraechinus_micropus/.

Perrone, Michael. "Adaptive Significance of Ear Tufts in Owls". *The Condor*, vol. 83, no. 4, Nov. 1981, p. 383. Crossref, https://doi.org/10.2307/1367512.

"Petaurista Philippensis (Indian Giant Flying Squirrel)". *Animal Diversity Web*, https://animaldiversity.org/accounts/Petaurista_philippensis/.

"Platacanthomys Lasiurus". *Earthpedia*, https://earthpedia.earth.com/chordata/platacanthomyidae/platacanthomys-lasiurus/.

"Spot-Bellied Eagle-Owl". *eBird*, https://ebird.org/species/sbeowl1.

"Tylototriton Himalayanus". *AmphibiaWeb*, https://amphibiaweb.org/species/8429.

"Red Boa Factsheet." *WWF*, https://wwfin.awsassets.panda.org/downloads/red_sand_boa_factsheet__2021.pdf.

"Yunnan Newt Tylototriton verrucosus." *iNaturalist*, http://inaturalist.org/taxa/134982-Tylototriton-verrucosus.

Credits

Writer: Yamini Srikanth

Designer: Abhishikta Dutt

Picture Credits

iStockphoto: Banu R, 1484999958, 1500605857, 1494233698; ephotocorp, 1356534474, 1464051160, 1164854590, 1266946698, 1631192447, 1164896775, 1164854734, 1464050348, 2190335080, 1358737394; shabeerthurakkal, 653859046; Meet Poddar, 857715436, 857723666, 857696634, 857699952, 857696680; Lensalot, 1180781903, 1180781961; Soumabrata Moulick, 1431039010; neil bowman, 1444996800; Wirestock, 1463373684, 1459292795; reptiles4all, 580115014; fototrips, 871064580; JasonOndreicka, 904944238; Tanes Ngamsom, 945997168, 1158220125; Ramyasshree Ramaswamy, 2188867874; mtreasure, 1456367292; sham prakash, 1235596399, 1235596405.

Wikimedia Commons: Owl in Trivandrum zoo by Mithun.M.Das; Petaurista philippensis Kalyan Varma; Indian giant flying squirrel by Kalyan Varma; Indian giant flying squirrelby Pratik Jain; Indian giant flying squirrel by Vickey Chauhan; hump-nosed viper by Nativeplants garden; greater short-nosed bat by J.M. Garg; Short-nosed Indian Fruit Bat by Shantanu Kuveskar; short-nosed bat harem by Rajesh Puttaswamaiah; short-nosed bat by PO Nameer; Malabar spiny dormouse by davidraju; Asian palm civet by Tisha Mukherjee; Krokodilmolch by Wilfried Berns; Ocypode ceratophthalmus by Afsar Nayakkan; Ocypode ceratophthalmus bypalmfly; ghost crab by Ganesh Mohan T; juvenile red sand boa by Jayendra Chiplunkar; Red Sand Boa Eryx johnii by Ashahar alias Krishna Khan.

iNaturalist: Spot-bellied eagle-owl by kalyanvarma; Spot-bellied eagle-owl byjoelcorrea7777; Spot-bellied eagle-owl by surabhi_srivastava_gaur; Indian hedgehog by ashwinv; Malabar spiny dormouse by kalyanvarma; Malabar spiny dormouse by ansilbr; Malabar spiny dormouse by ramanarayanan.

Independent Sources: Spot-Bellied Eagle-owl pictures by Shashank Dalvi; palm civet photos by Dhritiman Mukherjee.

Map: Syailendra Gupta Muliawan, India Vectors by Vecteezy.

First published by Juggernaut Books 2025

Text copyright © Juggernaut Books 2025

10 9 8 7 6 5 4 3 2 1

P-ISBN: 9789353453824

E-ISBN: 9789353459390

All rights reserved. No part of this publication may be reproduced, transmitted, or stored in a retrieval system in any form or by any means without the written permission of the publisher.

Printed at Nutech Print Services - India